FROM DIXIE TO SWING

To access audio visit:
www.halleonard.com/mylibrary

Enter Code
2056-2837-0338-1820

ISBN 978-1-59615-441-4

EXCLUSIVELY DISTRIBUTED BY

HAL•LEONARD®

7777 W. BLUEMOUND RD. P.O. BOX 13819 MILWAUKEE, WI 53213

Visit Hal Leonard Online at
www.halleonard.com

Way Down Yonder In New Orleans

TRUMPET

Words and Music by
HENRY CREAMER
J. TURNER LAYTON

4

Red Sails In The Sunset

Words and Music by
JIMMY KENNEDY
HUGH WILLIAMS
(WILL GROSZ)

On The Sunny Side Of The Street

Words and Music by
DOROTHY FIELDS
JIMMY McHUGH

Second Hand Rose

Words and Music by
GRANT CLARKE
JAMES F. HANLEY

TRUMPET

never get a single thing that's new._____

E - ven Jake the plum - ber, he's the man I a - dore,_____ He

had the nerve to tell me he's been mar - ried be - fore,_____

Ev - 'ry - one knows____ that I'm just Sec - ond Hand Rose____ From

Sec - ond Av - e - nue,_____ From

Sec - ond Av - e - nue._____

Trombone Solo

Take 4 bars rest,
then repeat last 4 bars

Royal Garden Blues

Words and Music by
CLARENCE WILLIAMS
SPENCER WILLIAMS

TRUMPET

♩ = 232

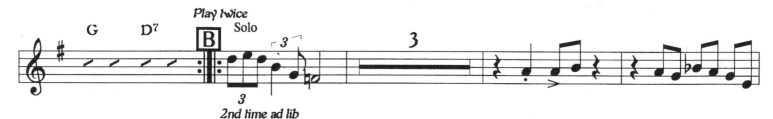

9

ROSE OF WASHINGTON SQUARE

Words and Music by
BALLARD McDONALD
JAMES F. HANLEY

I Want A Little Girl

Words and Music by
BILLY MOLL
MURRAY MENCHER

TRUMPET

Exactly Like You

Words and Music by
DOROTHY FIELDS
JIMMY McHUGH

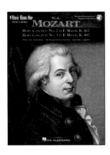